ANIMAL JOURNEYS

Carron Brown

Illustrated by Carrie May

Kane Miller
A DIVISION OF EDC PUBLISHING

Many animals make incredible journeys
every year, month, and even each day.
This is called migration.

Some migrate to find food, water, and
warmer weather. Others travel to find
a safe place to have their young.

Shine a flashlight behind the page
or hold it to the light to reveal
different animals on their travels.
Discover a world of great surprises.

We're at the top of the world.

This is Mount Everest,
the highest mountain
on our planet.

What's hiding behind
the clouds?

Bar-headed geese fly high in the sky on a 1,700-mile journey.

In Spring, the geese fly north from India to China and Mongolia to have their goslings.

In the fall, they return to India for the winter.

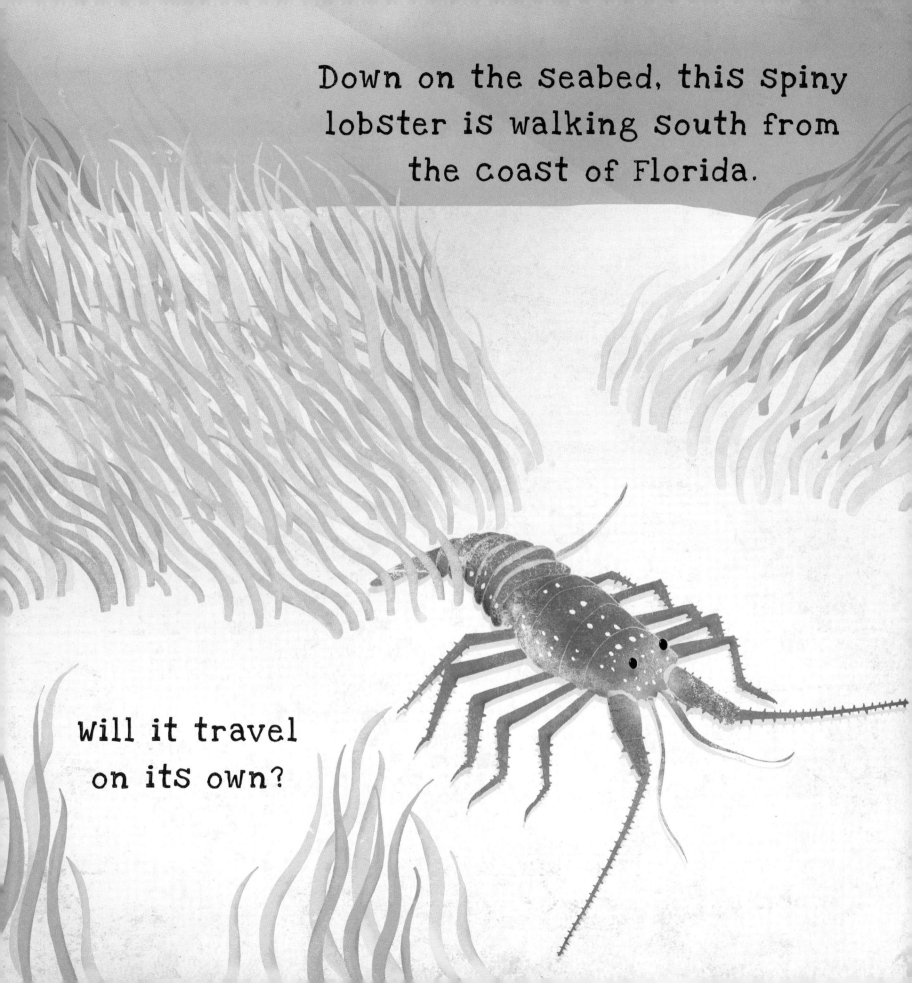

Down on the seabed, this spiny lobster is walking South from the coast of Florida.

Will it travel on its own?

No, there's a line of lobsters,
all traveling together.

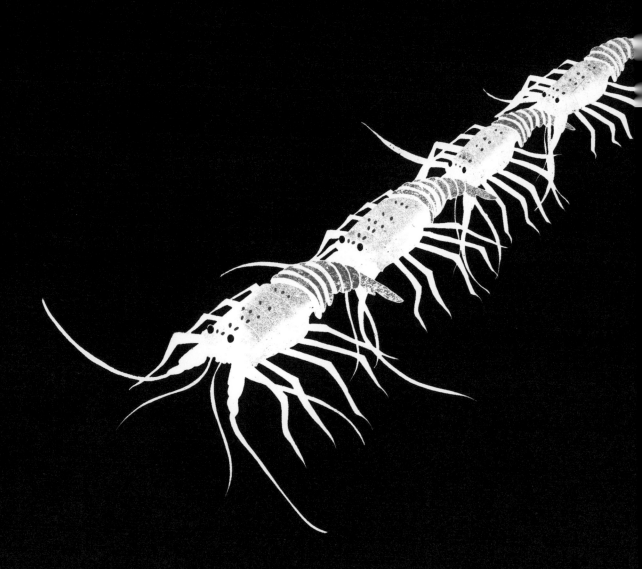

Every fall, these lobsters make their
way to reefs in deeper, warmer water.
They march back to the shallows in spring.

These blue wildebeest are leaping into the Mara River. They are traveling from the Serengeti in Tanzania to the Masai Mara reserve in Kenya.

What's lurking in the water?

Crocodiles lie in wait.

Up to two million
wildebeest make this
dangerous crossing
twice a year, following
the seasonal rains.

Where there's rain,
there's lots of green
grass to eat!

Snap!

It's spring in Texas, and thousands of monarch butterflies have arrived. They flew here from Mexico, where they stayed warm over the winter.

What's under this leaf?

A chrysalis.

Inside, a new butterfly is growing.
This new generation will migrate
farther north for the summer.

Each year, it takes four
generations of monarch
butterflies to make the full
migration, from Mexico to
the northeastern US and back.

This gray whale is rising to take a big, deep breath. She's traveled to the waters of Baja California in Mexico from the Arctic, where she has been feeding all summer.

Why has she swum here?

The water here is shallow and warm—
perfect for having her calf!

Gray whales make one
of the longest mammal
migrations. They swim
about 12,000 miles—
from the Arctic to
Mexico and back.

On this beach in Hawaii, a green sea turtle is slowly crawling to the ocean.

What has she left in the sand?

Eggs!

She has laid and carefully buried
about one hundred of them.

Green sea turtles return
to the same beach every
few years to lay their
eggs. The journey is
about 600 miles.

This Arctic tern is hovering
over the ocean.

What's it looking at?

A Shoal of fish!

These birds have a long journey, and
tasty fish help provide energy.

Every winter, they fly South
to Antarctica where it's warmer.
In Spring, they return to the Arctic
to raise their chicks. There and back,
the journey is about 50,000 miles!

A herd of porcupine caribou is on the move after spending Spring and Summer on the northern Alaskan coast.

Who's making their first journey?

It's a calf.

Porcupine caribou have their young in the spring. In the fall, when the calves are old enough, the herd travels to Canada to find food.

They travel almost 3,000 miles every year—the longest land migration of all animals!

The moon is shining over the ocean.

Many animals are tucked away for the night,
but who is rising from the deep?

A squid!

Every night, all over the world, squid
swim up from the dark ocean depths.

It's safer for them to feed at this time
when many other predators are asleep.

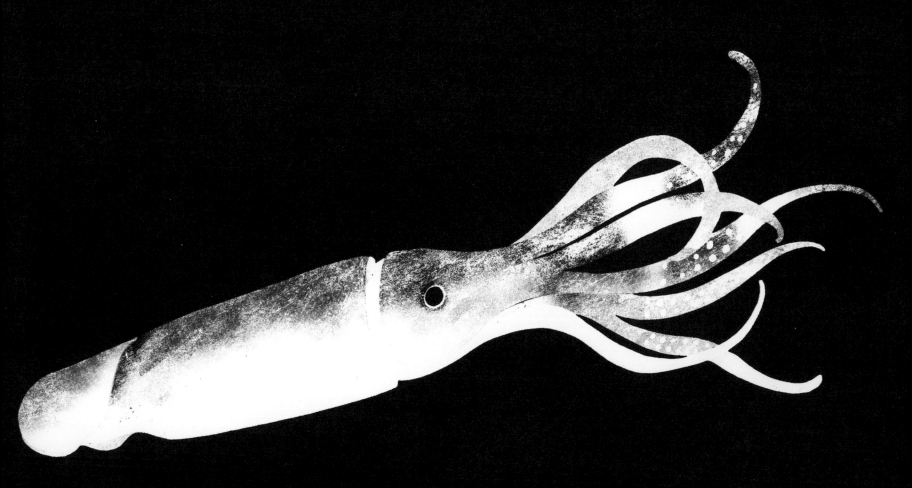

A road is closed on Christmas Island,
a small island in the Indian Ocean.

ROAD
CLOSED

What's this family
looking at?

Red crabs are crossing the road.

Every year, between October and December,
millions of these crabs scurry across
the island to the sea to release their eggs.

Many roads are closed to traffic
so the crabs can travel safely.

Hungry brown bears sit and stand in a river in Maine.

What are they waiting for?

Atlantic salmon are a tasty meal.

The fish are swimming
up the river.

Swipe!

They've traveled over 6,000 miles
from the Atlantic Ocean to lay
eggs at the same place where
they hatched.

It's winter, and these northern elephant seals are basking on a beach in California.

Why do they come here?

To have their pups!

Then, in Spring, they swim to Alaska to feed.
They return to California in the summer to
shed their outer skin. This is called molting.

Once they've molted, they
head north to feed again,
traveling a total of 13,000
miles every year.

Every year, the trees in Kasanka National Park, Zambia, become home to about 10 million fruit bats. They fly in from all over Africa between October and December.

Why are they here?

To feed! Each night, they
fly to find fruit to eat.

Their journey to the park is the
world's largest mammal migration.

In Antarctica, three emperor penguins waddle and slide across the ice.

Where are they going?

They are traveling south to their
nesting grounds.

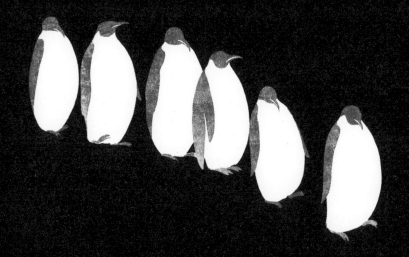

The whole colony is
following behind!

Emperor penguins march up to 100 miles
inland from the sea to lay their eggs
and rear their chicks.

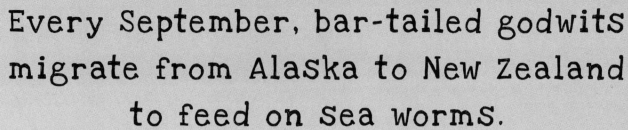

Every September, bar-tailed godwits migrate from Alaska to New Zealand to feed on sea worms.

The journey is a 7,500-mile flight across the Pacific Ocean without any stops.

How do we know this?

By tracking!

Scientists have attached special
satellite trackers to the birds,
which record their journeys.

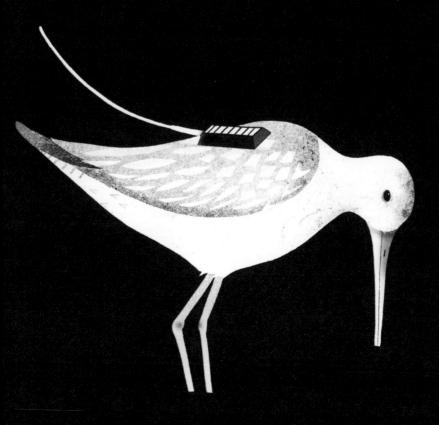

Now that you've read about these amazing journeys, look for animals on their travels near you. Do you see some animals at only certain times of the year? It may be that they have traveled from far away.

The next time you see them, wish them luck on their journey.

There's more...

Animals that migrate have incredible ways to cope with their long journeys. Here are some of the methods animals use to travel safely.

Flying in formation
Large migrating birds fly in a "V" shape, with one bird taking the lead at the front. This helps the whole flock fly faster and easier because the lead bird breaks up the air, which gives extra lift to the birds behind it. The birds take turns being the leader.

Sticking together
Many animals migrate together instead of traveling alone. Animals that eat other animals (predators) think twice about attacking a large group. It also helps the migrating animals to stay warm because they can huddle together while they rest.

Being prepared
Some animals build up their bodies before they migrate, making sure they have enough energy for many days of travel. The bar-tailed godwit doubles its weight in fat and grows new, strong flight feathers before taking off on its long journey.

Sleeping on the move

Arctic terns and some other migratory birds can sleep while flying, gliding while taking short naps. Arctic terns also eat while flying.

Finding the way

Migrating animals have different methods for reaching their destinations. Scientists believe some birds use the stars to navigate, wildebeest follow the scent of rain, while salmon remember the smell of the stream where they were hatched. Sea turtles can even sense changes in the Earth's magnetic field, which helps them find their way.

Changing routes

Animals sometimes need to change their route to survive a migration. They may do this if the land has been damaged, such as by a fire or a flood. They will travel to where they can find the best food to eat.

First American Edition 2022
Kane Miller, A Division of EDC Publishing

Copyright © 2022 Quarto Publishing plc

For information contact:
Kane Miller, A Division of EDC Publishing
5402 S 122nd E Ave, Tulsa, OK 74146
www.kanemiller.com
www.myubam.com

Library of Congress Control Number: 2021953173

Manufactured in Huizhou City, Guangdong, China TT072022

ISBN: 978-1-68464-518-3

1 2 3 4 5 6 7 8 9 10

FSC
www.fsc.org

MIX
Paper from
responsible sources
FSC® C016973